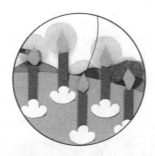

To brave firefighters everywhere
—J. Marzollo

For Maddie and Andy
—J. Moffatt

Text copyright © 1996 by Jean Marzollo.
Illustrations copyright © 1996 by Judith Moffatt.
All rights reserved. Published by Scholastic Inc.
Printed in the U.S.A.

ISBN 0-439-45163-9

SCHOLASTIC, HELLO READER!, CARTWHEEL BOOKS, and associated logos
and designs are trademarks and/or registered trademarks of Scholastic Inc.

10 9   40   11 10

I Am Fire

by Jean Marzollo
Illustrated by Judith Moffatt

SCHOLASTIC INC.

New York   Toronto   London   Auckland   Sydney
Mexico City   New Delhi   Hong Kong   Buenos Aires

Fire heats your soup.

Fire warms your rooms.

Fire lights your life.

But watch out!
Fire can be harmful.

Children can help to
prevent fires.
If you find matches,
give them to a grown-up.
Do not try to light them.

Watch fireworks with a grown-up. Stay way back.

Fire is hot.
Don't touch fire.
Don't touch hot things.
Just look.

Practice fire drills
at home.

Have a place to meet.

Practice fire drills
at school, too.

If you see a fire start,
tell a grown-up quickly.

If you are inside a building that's on fire, go out.

If there is smoke, crawl under it. Stay low and go. Don't go back inside.

If your clothes are on fire,
stop where you are.
Drop to the ground.
Roll over and over to smother
the flames.
Remember these three words.
Stop. Drop. Roll.

If you want to know more
about fire, ask a grown-up.

Learn how to call the fire department where you live.